FILM HITS

Music arranged and processed by Barnes Music Engraving Ltd, East Sussex TN22 4HA, England
Cover design by xheight Limited
Published 1996

IMP

ALFIE

Words by HAL DAVID
Music by BURT BACHARACH

Registration
Upper: Orch. Strings / Solo Harmonica (or Piano)
Lower: Strings / Piano
Pedal: 8' Acoustic Bass
Rhythm 16 Beat (or 8 Beat)
Tempo ♩ = 70

ARTHUR'S THEME
(Best That You Can Do)

Words and Music by BURT BACHARACH, CAROLE BAYER SAGER,
CHRISTOPHER CROSS and PETER ALLEN

Registration
Upper: Pop Organ or Electric Piano
Lower: Electric Piano (add Strings on Chorus)
Pedal: 8' Electric Bass
Rhythm 8 Beat
Tempo ♩ = 112

Once in your life you'll find ___ her,
Ar-thur, he does what he pleas - es,

some-one who turns ___ your
all of his life, ___ his

heart a - round, and
mas - ter's toys, and

next thing you know, you're
deep in his heart, he's

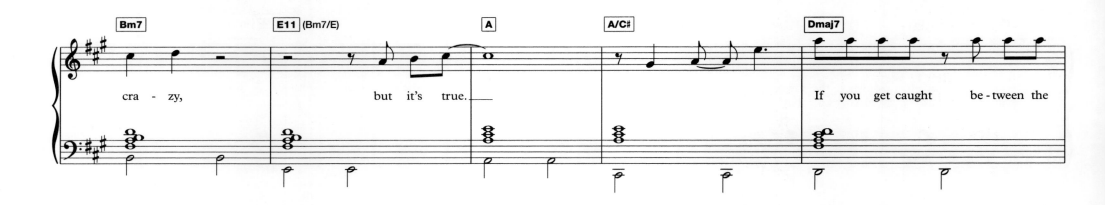

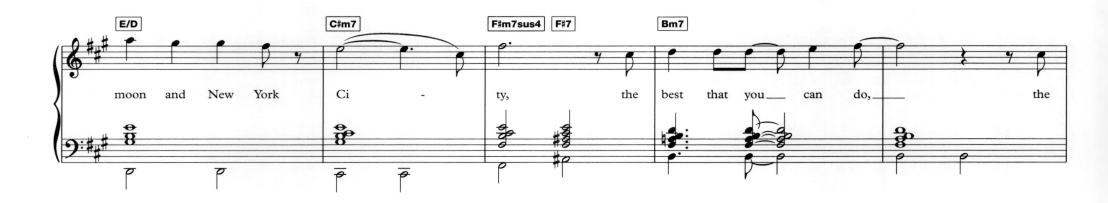

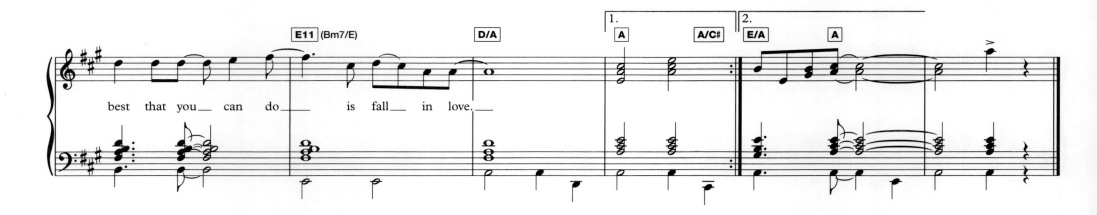

BIG SPENDER

Words by DOROTHY FIELDS
Music by CY COLEMAN

Registration
Upper: Brass
Lower: Piano / Brass
Pedal: 8' Acoustic Bass
Rhythm   Swing or Shuffle
Tempo   ♩ = 120

11

BRIGHT EYES

Words and Music by MIKE BATT

Registration
Upper: Solo Flute / Strings
Lower: Strings / Electric Piano
Pedal: 8' Acoustic Bass
Rhythm 8 Beat or Beguine
Tempo ♩ = 118

13

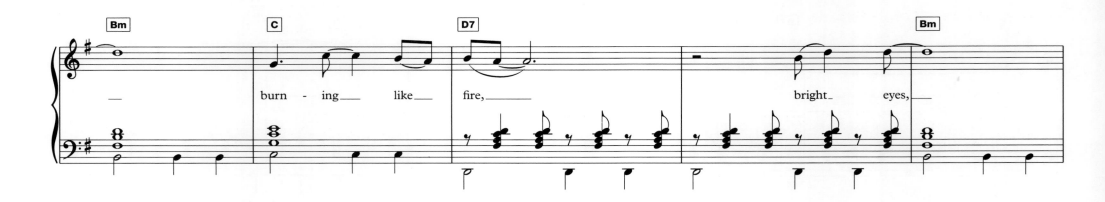

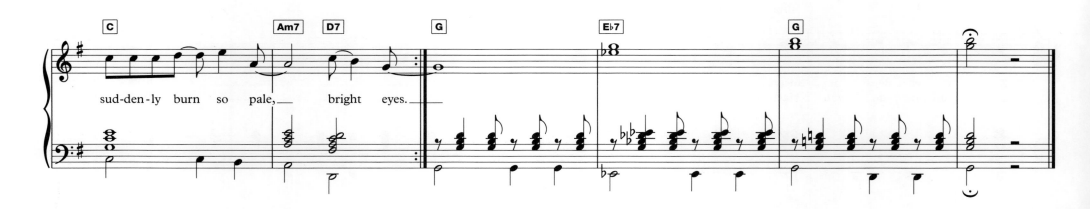

ENDLESS LOVE

Words and Music by LIONEL RICHIE

Registration
Upper: Piano or Electric Piano
Lower: Strings / Choirs
Pedal: 8' Acoustic Bass
Rhythm 16 Beat
Tempo ♩ = 85

EVERGREEN

Words by PAUL WILLIAMS
Music by BARBRA STREISAND

Registration
Upper: Strings or Piano
Lower: Electric Piano / Organ
Pedal: 8' Acoustic Bass
Rhythm Rhumba or 8 Beat
Tempo ♩ = 98

Love, soft as an ea - sy chair, love, fresh as the morn - ing air. One love that is

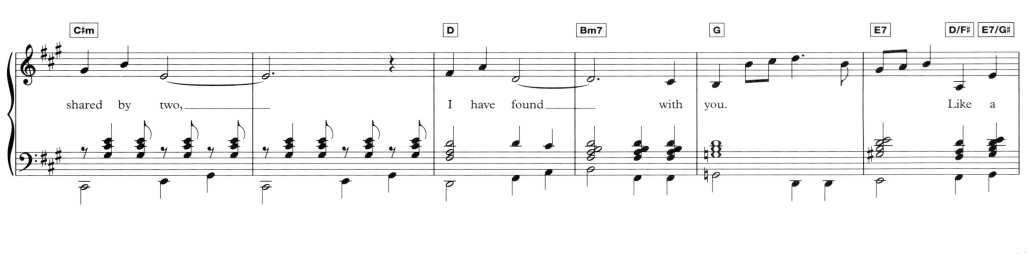

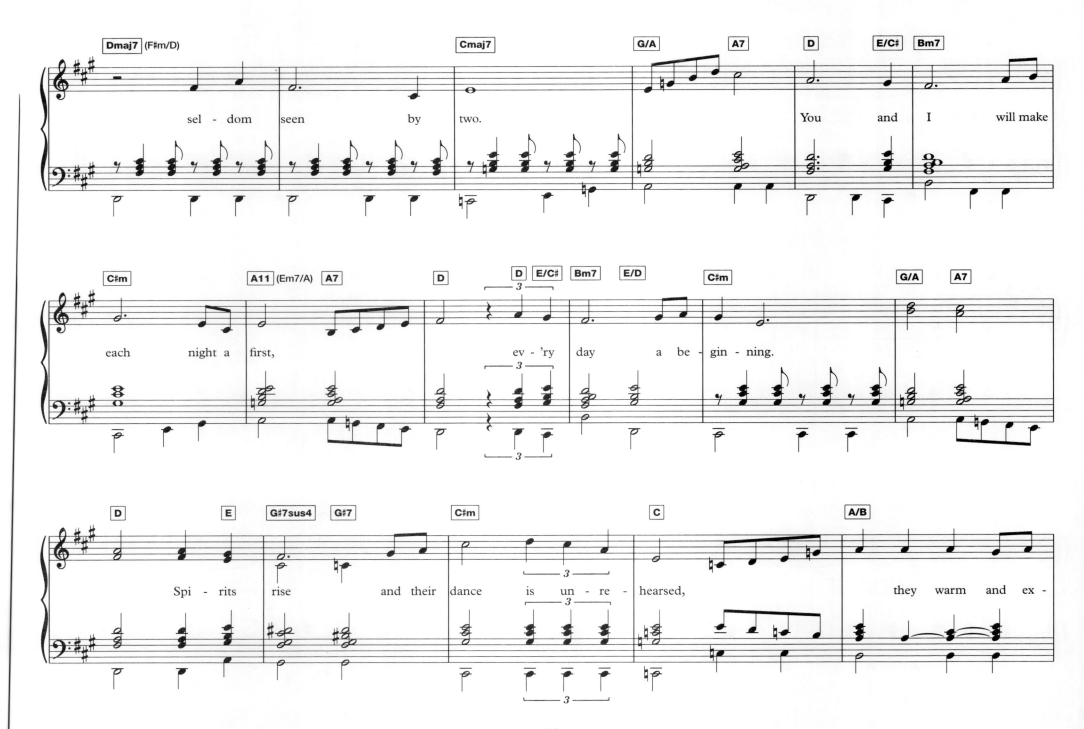

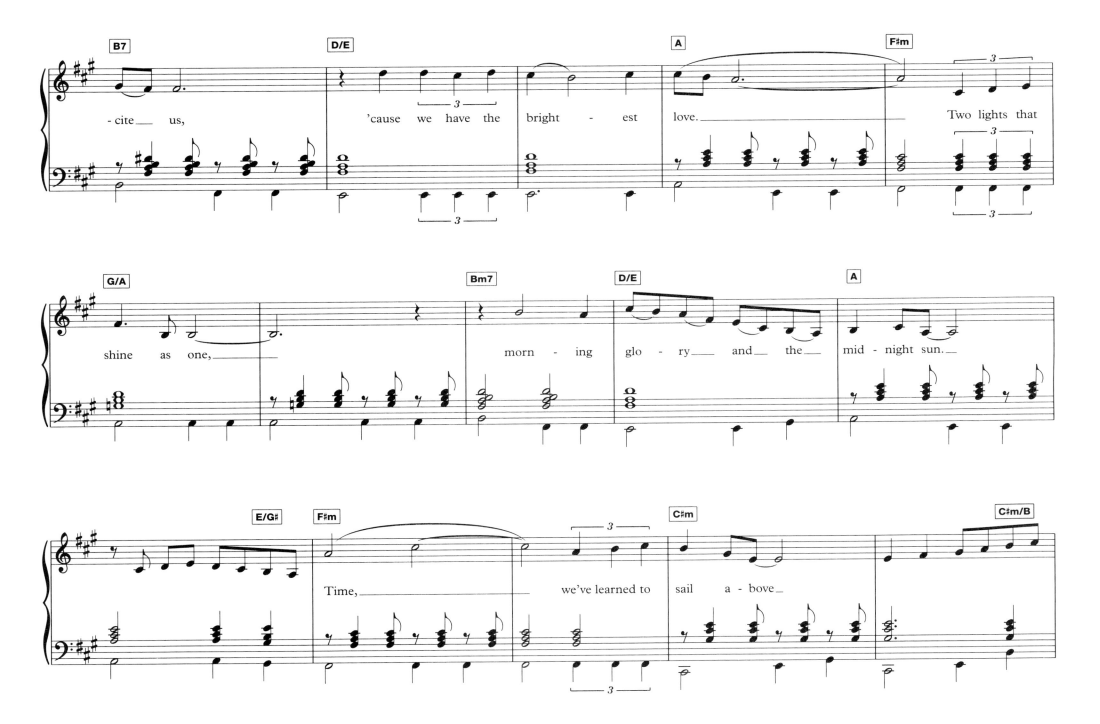

FOR YOUR EYES ONLY

Words by MICHAEL LEESON
Music by BILL CONTI

Registration
Upper: Synth Brass
Lower: Brass / Strings
Pedal: 8' or 16' Electric Bass
Rhythm 8 Beat
Tempo ♩ = 86

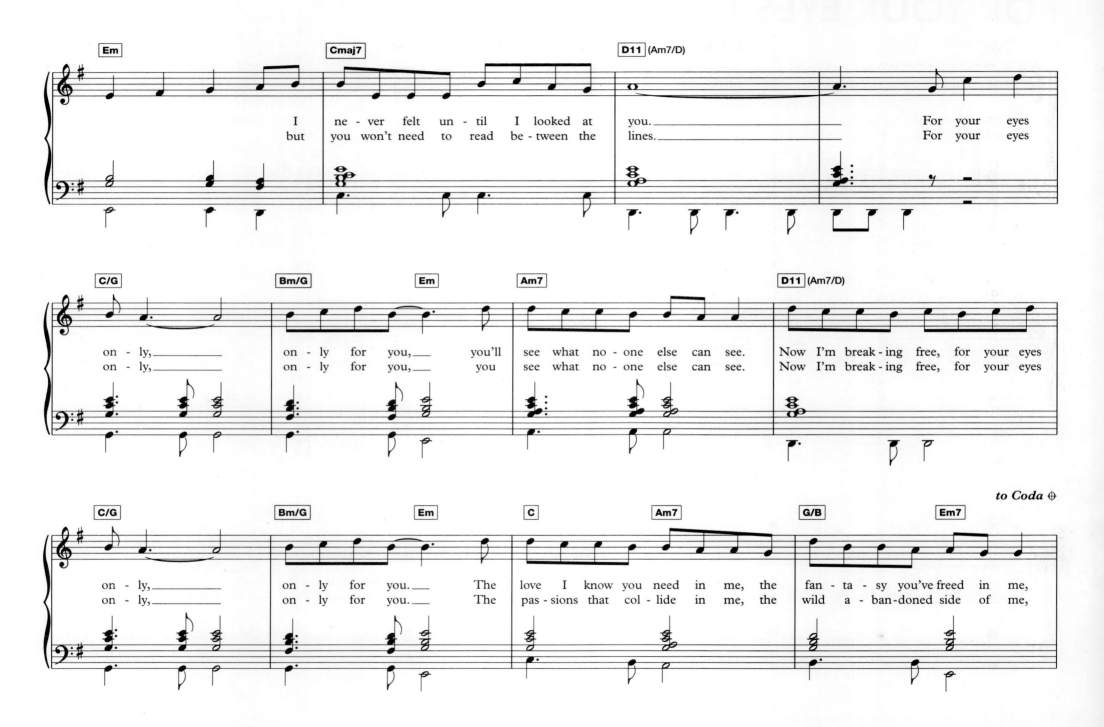

24

(I'VE HAD) THE TIME OF MY LIFE

Words and Music by FRANKIE PREVITE, JOHN DE NICOLA and DONALD MARKOWITZ

Registration	
Upper:	Electric Guitar / Brass or Organ
Lower:	Guitar / Strings
Pedal:	8' Electric Bass
Rhythm	Disco
Tempo	♩ = 120

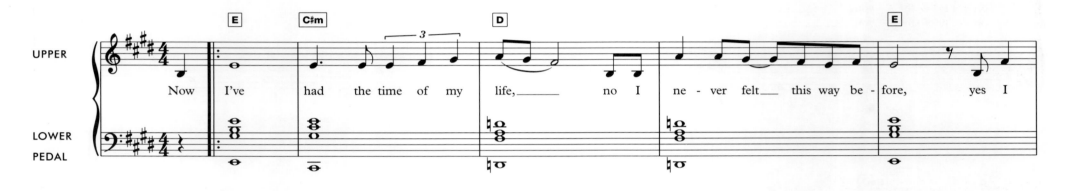

27

28

29

I HAVE NOTHING

Words and Music by LINDA THOMPSON-JENNER and DAVID FOSTER

Registration
Upper: Piano / Electric Piano
Lower: Piano / Strings
Pedal: 8' Electric Bass
Rhythm   Slow Rock 12/8
Tempo   ♪. = 50

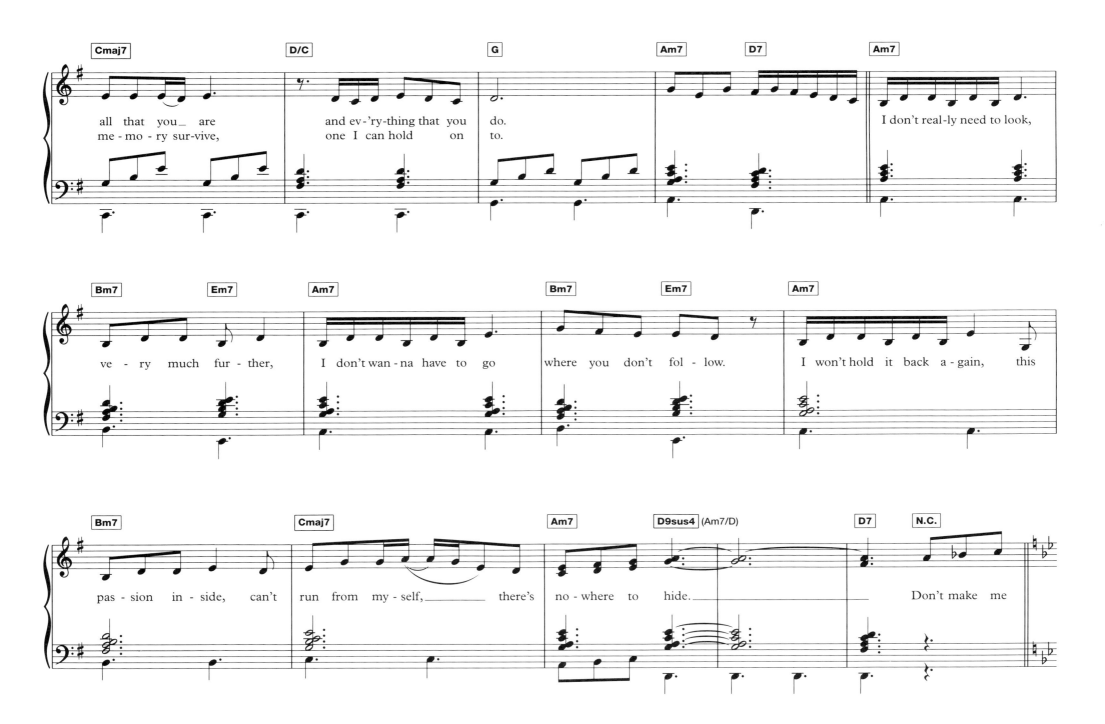

LA BAMBA

Words and Music by RICHIE VALENS

Registration
Upper: Brass
Lower: Brass / Piano
Pedal: Electric Bass
Rhythm   Latin Rock or 8 beat
Tempo   ♩ = 125

RAINDROPS KEEP FALLIN' ON MY HEAD

Words by HAL DAVID
Music by BURT BACHARACH

Registration
Upper: Pop Organ / Vibraphone
Lower: Piano / Strings / Organ
Pedal: 8' Acoustic Bass
Rhythm   Swing or Bounce
Tempo   ♩ = 108

THE SOUND OF MUSIC

Words by OSCAR HAMMERSTEIN II
Music by RICHARD RODGERS

Registration
Upper: Strings or Organ / Strings
Lower: Electric Piano / Strings
Pedal: 8' Acoustic Bass
Rhythm   Beguine or Rhumba
Tempo   ♩ = 98

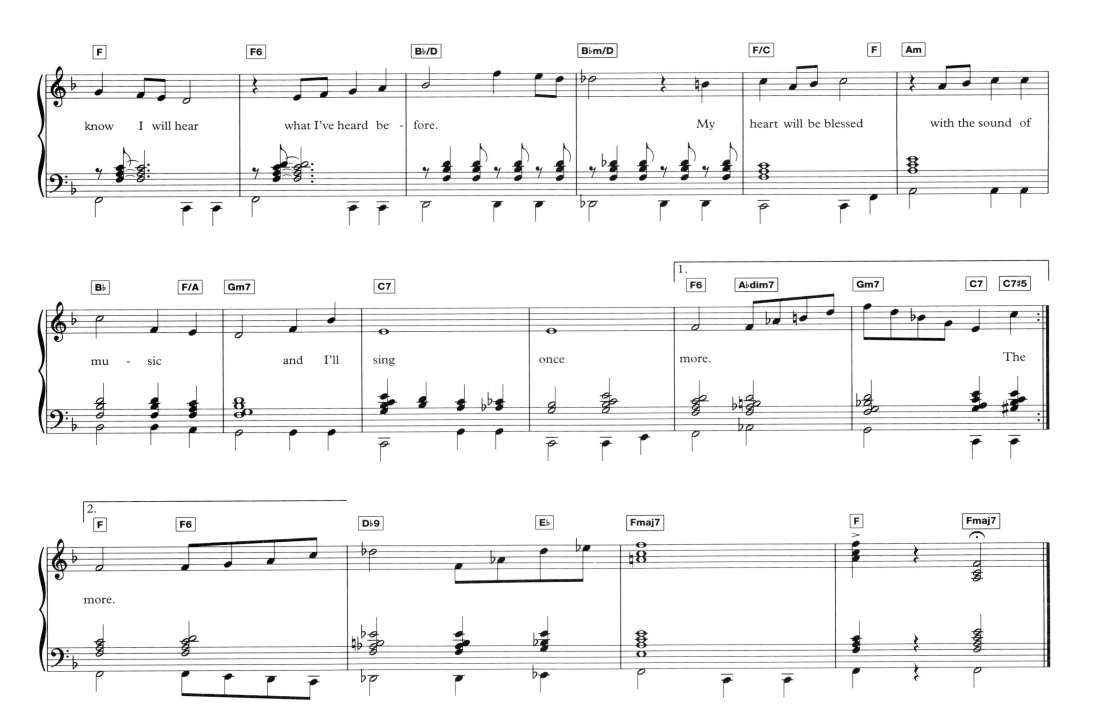

STAR WARS (Main Title)

JOHN WILLIAMS

Registration
Upper: Brass / Trumpets
Lower: Brass / Strings
Pedal: 8' Electric Bass Guitar
Rhythm   6/8 March or 8 beat
Tempo   ♩ = 110

TARA'S THEME

MAX STEINER

Registration
Upper: Orch. Strings
Lower: Strings / Piano
Pedal: Acoustic Bass or String Bass
Rhythm Latin (Bossa Nova or Beguine)
Tempo ♩ = 100

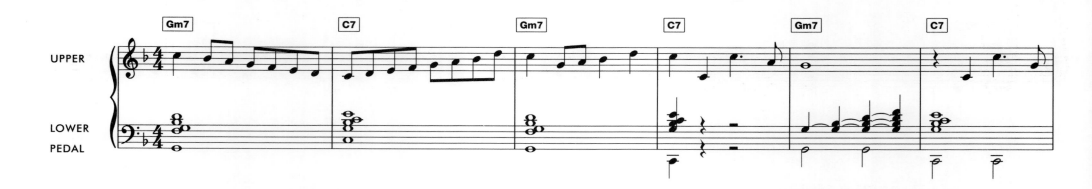

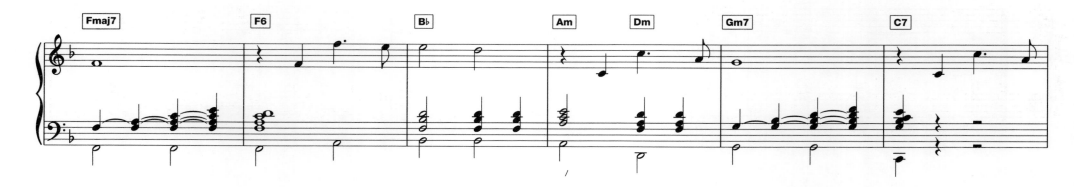

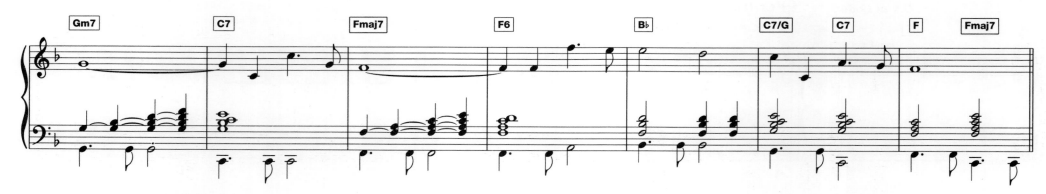

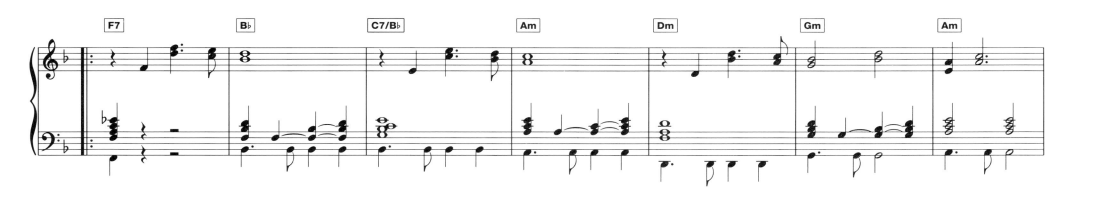

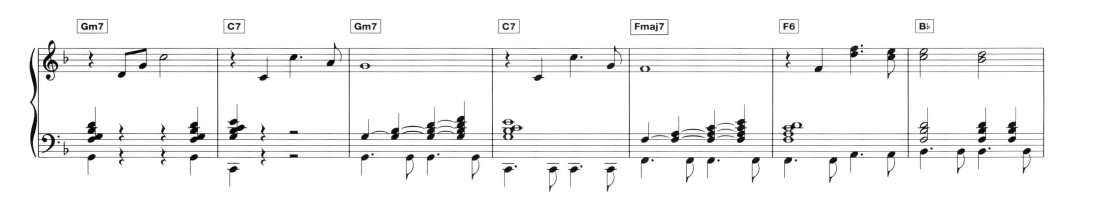

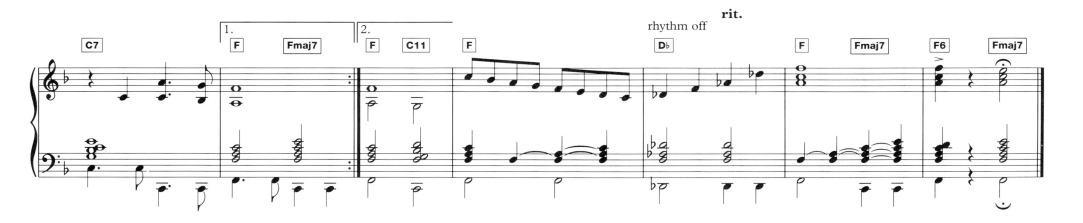

SUMMER HOLIDAY

Words and Music by BRUCE WELCH and BRIAN BENNETT

Registration
Upper: Electric Guitar
Lower: Electric Piano / Strings
Pedal: 8' Electric Bass
Rhythm   Rock Shuffle
Tempo   ♩ = 110

47

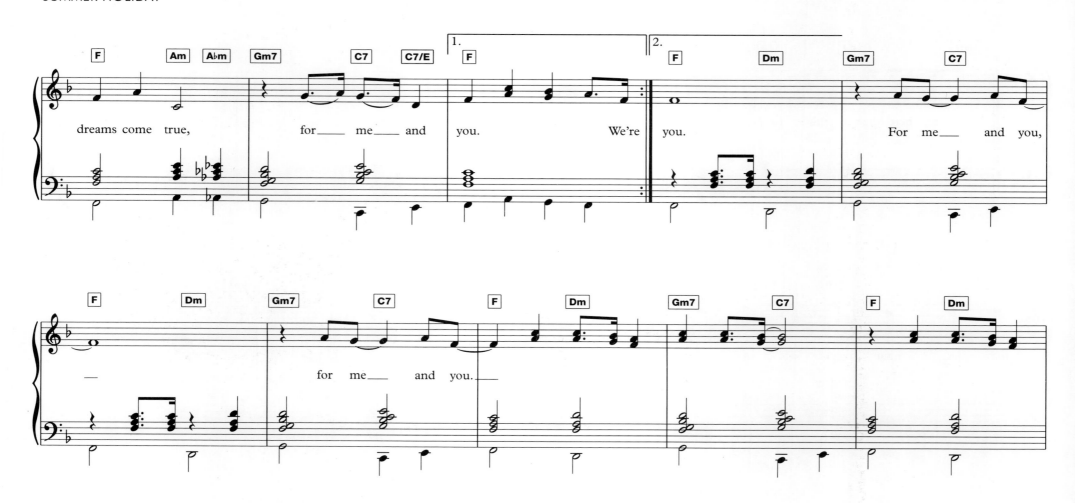

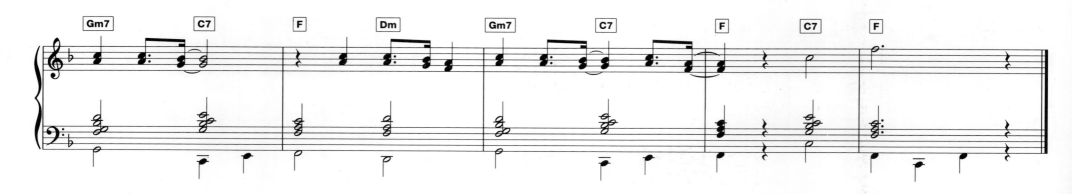

Printed in England
Panda Press · Haverhill · Suffolk · 2/96